D1402834

Lots of things you want to know about
ASTRONAUTS
...and some you don't!

Written and
Illustrated by
David West

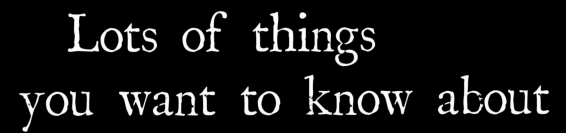

A⁺
Smart Apple Media

Published by Smart Apple Media, an imprint of Black Rabbit Books
P.O. Box 3263, Mankato, Minnesota 56002
www.smartapplemedia.com

Produced by David West 👥 Children's Books
6 Princeton Court, 55 Felsham Road, London SW15 1AZ

Designed and illustrated by David West

Copyright © 2013 David West Children's Books

Library of Congress Cataloging-in-Publication Data

West, David, 1956-
Lots of things you want to know about astronauts ...and some you don't! / David West.
pages cm
Includes index.
ISBN 978-1-62588-088-8
1. Manned space flight–History–Juvenile literature. 2. Astronauts–Juvenile literature. I. Title. II. Title:
Astronauts.
TL793.W4693 2015
629.45–dc23

2013030714

Printed in China
CPSIA compliance information DWCB15CP
311214

9 8 7 6 5 4 3 2 1

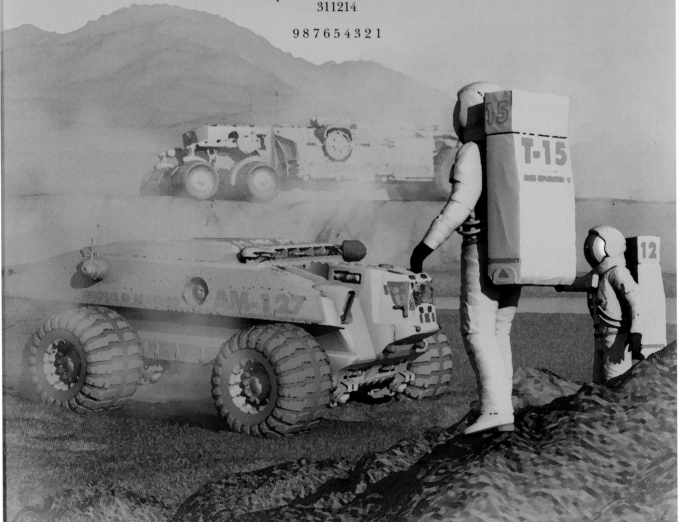

Contents

The First Astronaut Was a Dog

Before people were sent into space, scientists had little idea of how spaceflight would affect living things. So spacecraft were launched into space using animals. In 1957, the first animal to **orbit** the planet was a stray dog from the streets of Moscow.

Her name was Laika, which means "barker" in Russian. Unfortunately Laika didn't survive the journey.

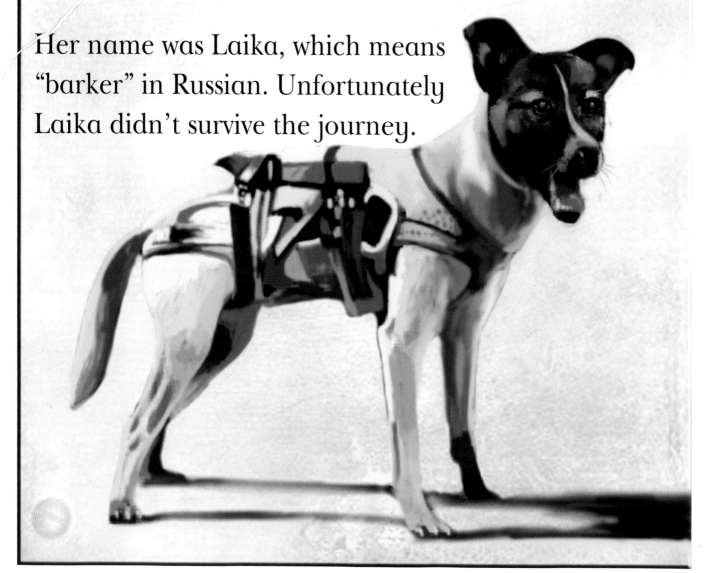

The First Person in Space Was a Cosmonaut

Soviet spacemen are called cosmonauts, which means "universe sailor." In 1961 a **Soviet** pilot named Yuri Gagarin made the first journey into outer space. He made a complete orbit of the Earth in Vostok 1 before landing safely back on Earth.

Early Spacecraft Had Room for Only One Astronaut

A month after Yuri Gagarin's epic flight, Alan Shepard became the first American in space in "Freedom 7." Because of their small size, it was said that the Mercury spacecraft, including "Faith 7" and "Friendship 7," were worn, not ridden.

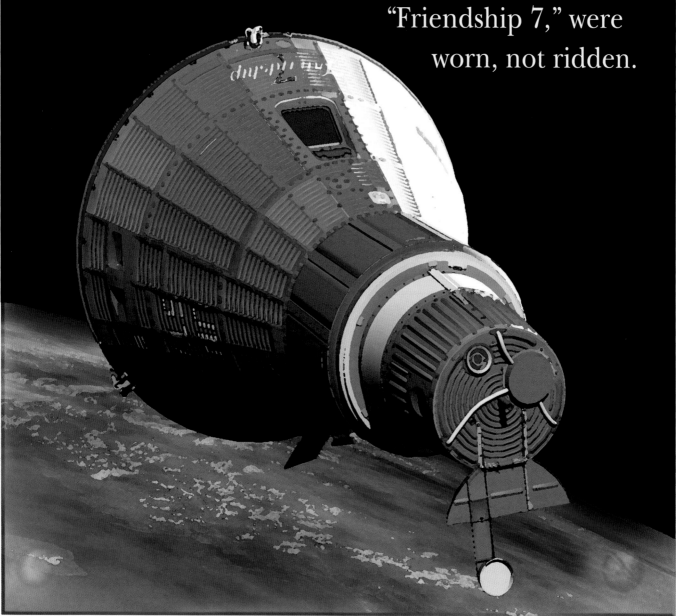

Giant Rockets Fire Spaceships into Space

To escape the Earth's **gravity**, large rockets are needed to get astronauts into space. The largest were the Saturn V rockets. They were 363 feet (110.6 m) tall and weighed 6.2 million pounds (2,800 metric tons). That's as much as 450 elephants!

Russian Spacecraft Landed with a Bump

After reentering Earth's atmosphere, returning spacecraft deploy a parachute. This slows their rate of speed. Russian Soyuz capsules fire rockets seconds before landing to soften touchdown on the hard earth of Kazakhstan.

American Spacecraft Landed with a Splash

Before the Space Shuttle was built, returning American space capsules landed in the ocean. After splashdown, the spacecraft was rescued by a helicopter, which hoisted it aboard an aircraft carrier. Later, the crew was lifted from the capsule before it was airlifted back to a ship.

An Eagle Landed on the Moon

Launched by a Saturn V rocket on July 16, 1969, Apollo 11 was the fifth manned mission of NASA's Apollo program. On July 20, the **Lunar Module**, known as the "Eagle," landed on the Moon. Six hours later, Neil Armstrong stepped onto the Moon.

You Can Jump Higher on the Moon

Astronauts who visited the Moon found that they had to move in shuffling bunny hops. This is because the Moon's gravity is weaker than Earth's. Astronauts could jump about six times higher on the Moon than they could on Earth!

Astronauts Went for a Drive on the Moon

When Apollo 15 astronauts touched down on the Moon, they had an extra-special tool packed away on their lunar lander. It was a lunar rover that enabled them to become the first people ever to drive on the surface of the Moon.

Apollo 13 Missed the Moon

56 hours into their trip to the Moon, the astronauts of Apollo 13 heard a loud bang, followed by thrusters firing to correct the spaceship's position. An oxygen bottle had exploded in the **Service Module**. The crew had to cancel the Moon landing and use the Lunar Module as a lifeboat. They had to travel around the Moon before returning safely back to Earth.

The Space Shuttle Was a Reusable Spacecraft

The Space Shuttle was used on a total of 135 missions from 1981 to 2011, all launched from the Kennedy Space Center in Florida. The vehicle consisted of a spaceplane for orbit and re-entry, fueled by an external fuel tank, with reusable, strap-on solid booster rockets.

The boosters returned to Earth by parachute, and the spaceplane glided back after reentering Earth's atmosphere. The external fuel tank burned up in the atmosphere after it was **jettisoned**.

Five spaceplanes, Columbia, Challenger, Discovery, Atlantis, and Endeavour were built. Two, Challenger and Columbia, were destroyed in accidents. Their entire crews were killed.

Astronauts Put a Telescope in Space

Space Shuttles completed many major missions. They launched numerous satellites and probes to planets. They also helped astronauts conduct experiments and construct and service the International Space Station. In 1990, a Space Shuttle carried the Hubble Space Telescope into orbit. This telescope remains in operation today.

Space Suits Are Like Mini Spaceships

Outer space is a vacuum with extremes in temperature. The space suit keeps astronauts safe, supplying them with oxygen, suitable pressure, temperature regulation, a communication system, and waste management (toilet facility). There is even a strap-on rocket pack that allows the astronaut to move around just like a spacecraft.

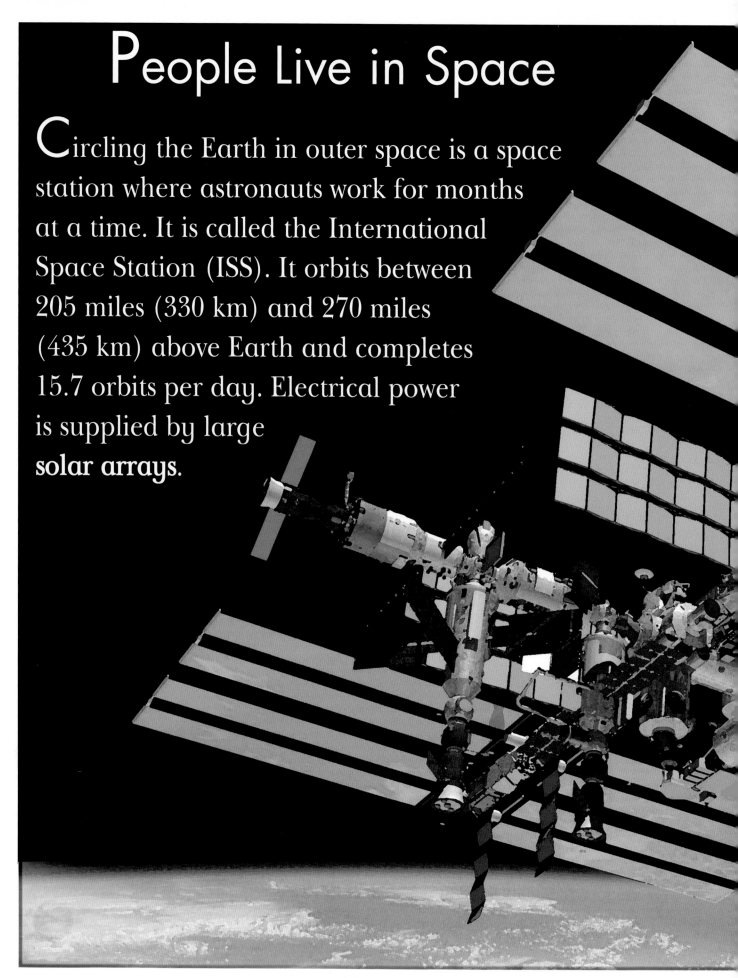

People Live in Space

Circling the Earth in outer space is a space station where astronauts work for months at a time. It is called the International Space Station (ISS). It orbits between 205 miles (330 km) and 270 miles (435 km) above Earth and completes 15.7 orbits per day. Electrical power is supplied by large **solar arrays**.

Tourists Visit the ISS

Astronauts and supplies are brought to and from the space station by Soyuz spacecraft. Sometimes seats are available and sold to "space tourists" for around $40 million.

Astronauts' Taste Buds Don't Work as Well in Space

A special effort is made to make the food tasty on the ISS due to the reduced sense of taste in space. The **galley** has two food warmers, a refrigerator, and a water dispenser for heated and unheated water.

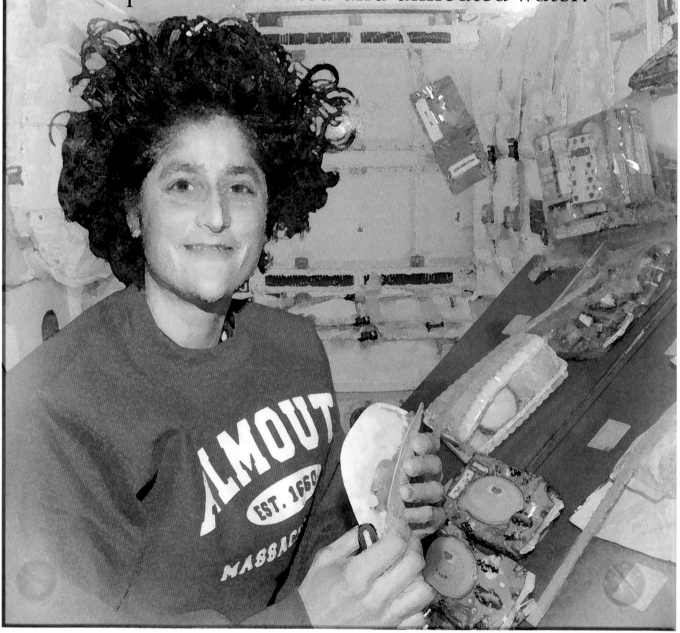

Astronauts Can Sleep Upside Down in Space

Because there is no gravity in space, there is no right way up. Astronauts can sleep in any direction. They need to be strapped into a sleeping bag that is attached to a wall so they don't float off. Sleeping in space is meant to be very easy and relaxing.

One Day Astronauts May Visit Planet Mars

Although many probes have successfully landed on Mars, humans have yet to make the trip. A trip to Mars and back would take 400 to 450 days, which is much longer than a year. In 2012, a private project named "Mars One" was announced, aiming to establish a settlement on Mars in 2023!

Glossary

galley the part of the space station where food is cooked and prepared

gravity the invisible force of a large object that pulls other objects toward it; the Earth's gravity keeps us from floating away

jettisoned dropped from a moving vehicle

Lunar Module the lander portion of the Apollo spacecraft which landed on the Moon

orbit the path of an object around a planet

probe an unmanned spacecraft that ventures to other planets and moons, or out into space

Service Module the part of a spacecraft that joins onto the Command Module; includes a rocket engine and provides electrical power and oxygen storage

solar array panels of special cells that convert sunlight into electricity

Soviet the name for anything Russian between 1922 and 1991

Index